AMERICAN PLURALISM AND THE COLLEGE CURRICULUM
HIGHER EDUCATION
IN A DIVERSE DEMOCRACY

THIS WORK WAS SUPPORTED BY A GRANT FROM THE
FORD FOUNDATION

Published by
Association of American Colleges and Universities
1818 R Street, NW
Washington, DC 20009

Copyright 1995

ISBN 0-911696-65-2
Library of Congress Catalog Card No. 95-80684

66309

TABLE OF CONTENTS

ACKNOWLEDGMENTS

The Association of American Colleges and Universities extends warm thanks to the Ford Foundation which provided grant support that enabled AAC&U to launch the American Commitments initiative and the work of the National Panel. We are especially grateful to Edgar Beckham, program officer in education and culture at the Ford Foundation, whose vision and commitment have helped hundreds of colleges and universities develop productive ways to educate students for the diversities and possibilities of the world they inherit. We also extend our thanks to Alison Bernstein, director of education and culture at the Ford Foundation, for her continuing confidence in AAC&U's work on equity and diversity. In addition, we thank the National Endowment for the Humanities (NEH) which has also supported the American Commitments initiative.

Thanks are due as well to Paula Brownlee, president of AAC&U, for her support of this initiative and for constructive readings of the Panel reports.

Members of the Panel owe great thanks to Maureen McNulty, who as special assistant to the Panel contributed editorial skill, bibliographical zeal, and organizational support to the work of the Panel. While Maureen McNulty was on maternity leave, Charlotte Hogsett ably served as editor-advisor to the project.

The curriculum recommendations presented in this report were developed by members of the National Panel. Troy Duster, Ramón Gutiérrez, Patrick Hill, Harry Kitano, Caryn McTighe Musil, Elizabeth Minnich, and Carol Schneider provided draft language for the recommendations. Carol Schneider, as scribe for the Panel, wrote the report.

In developing this report, the Panel benefited substantially from American Commitments' concurrent responsibility for a Curriculum and Faculty Development project on American pluralism in the curriculum involving ninety-three colleges and universities—twenty-two "resource institutions," and seventy-one "planning institutions." Panel member Caryn McTighe Musil and AAC&U senior fellow Gwen Dungy, who lead this major curriculum change initiative, helpfully connected it to the Panel's work.

Panel members and participants in the American Commitments Curriculum and Faculty Development project identified campus courses and programs that illustrate the recommendations. Maureen McNulty and Charlotte Hogsett elicited campus descriptions and wrote the examples. Kathleen Connelly, Kevin Hovland, Debra Humphreys, and Suzanne Hyers, all AAC&U staff members working on the American Commitments initiative, made very helpful contributions to the work of the Panel and of the Curriculum and Faculty Development project.

Drafts of this report were discussed with academic administrators and faculty members at AAC&U's 1995 annual meeting in Washington, D.C., and at two NEH-supported institutes at Williams College for participants in the Curriculum and Faculty Development project in August 1994 and July 1995. The report was also discussed with participants at the October 1994 fourth annual meeting of the Ford Foundation Campus Diversity Initiative in Tucson, at the October 1994 annual meeting of the Association for General and Liberal Studies in Savannah, at a March 1995 national conference on Teaching Cultural Encounters as General Education cosponsored by St. Lawrence University and AAC&U in New Orleans, and at an April 1995 national conference on Community, Difference, and Civic Engagement cosponsored by Grand Valley State University, the Kettering Foundation, and AAC&U in Chicago. We extend thanks to all who took part in these discussions and especially to participants who made written suggestions for strengthening the report.

Finally, we acknowledge the commitment, competence, and support of AAC&U's communications department, which prepared this report for publication. Joann Stevens, vice president for communications, helped develop the format for the reports and worked on the selection of cover photographs. Cindy Olson brought creativity, skill, and wonderful patience in creating the design for a report that remained in dialogue almost to the moment of publication. Thanks also to Amy Wajda and Heather Collins for their proofreading and copyediting.

THE AMERICAN COMMITMENTS NATIONAL PANEL

Suzanne Benally
Project Director,
The Institute on Ethnic Diversity,
Western Interstate Commission
for Higher Education

Alfred H. Bloom
President,
Swarthmore College

Johnnella Butler
Professor of American
Ethnic Studies,
University of Washington

Carlos Cortés
Professor of History,
University of California–Riverside

Bonnie Thornton Dill
Professor of Women's Studies,
University of Maryland

Troy Duster
Professor of Sociology,
University of California–Berkeley

Ramón Gutiérrez
Chair, Ethnic Studies Department,
University of California–San Diego

Patrick J. Hill
Professor of Interdisciplinary Study,
Evergreen State College

Harry H. Kitano
Professor of Social Welfare
and Sociology,
University of California–
Los Angeles

Lee Knefelkamp
Professor of Higher and Adult
Education,
Teachers College,
Columbia University

Elizabeth K. Minnich
Professor of Philosophy,
The Union Institute

Caryn McTighe Musil
Senior Research Associate,
Association of American Colleges
and Universities

Gayle Pemberton
Professor of African American
Studies,
Wesleyan University

Carol Schneider, ex officio
Executive Vice President, AAC&U,
Director, American Commitments
Initiative

Uri Treisman
Professor of Mathematics,
University of Texas–Austin

Frank Wong
Provost and Vice President
for Academic Affairs,
University of Redlands
*Frank Wong served as chair of the
National Panel until his untimely
death in April 1995.*

HIGHER EDUCATION AND THE CONTRADICTIONS OF AMERICAN PLURALISM

At the founding of this nation, proponents and opponents of the new Constitution engaged in a vigorous debate about the effects of societal diversity on the new political experiment. Speaking for the traditional view that successful republics must be small and homogeneous, the antifederalist Brutus argued, "In a republic, the manners, sentiments, and interests of the people should be similar. If this be not the case, there will be a constant clashing of opinions; and the representatives of one part will be continually striving against those of the other."

Against this conventional understanding of the prerequisites for a successful civic republic, the federalists argued that size and its resulting heterogeneity would prove a productive force in the vitality of the new republic. As Hamilton put it, the clash of contending views could strengthen the quality of public consideration and judgment (1982). The federalists won the argument and the nation embarked on a pathbreaking experiment in both diversity and republican self-government (Sunstein 1992).

This historic wager on the civic value of deliberation across difference led the framers to refuse constitutional proposals that representatives come to the Congress "instructed" on specific decisions by their respective constituencies. The insights to be gained through processes of dialogue and debate should not, they insisted, be impeded by prior restraints. Madison called for a "yielding and accommodating spirit," a willingness to change one's mind in the context of persuasive discussion. The First Amendment's protections for free speech both asserted and sought to assure the centrality of a vibrant public dialogue in the life of the young nation (Sunstein 1993).

SOCIAL HIERARCHIES

From the beginning then, the United States cast its lot both with heterogeneity as a defining characteristic and with dialogue and deliberation as democratic resources for the resolution of difference. Yet from the beginning as well, this historic commitment to a republic of reasoning was constrained and contradicted by the expectation that in this society founded on participatory citizenship, the citizens participating should be white and male.

The peoples who lived in the rapidly expanding United States were extraordinarily heterogeneous, culturally and racially. But from East to West, the nation's leaders acted assertively to restrict and control that diversity.

The Naturalization Act of 1790 enabled the extension of citizenship to immigrants, but restricted the privilege to persons who were white and male. American Indians were removed to special territories. Mexican Americans, following the conquest of their land, were politically and economically marginalized. The nation nearly sundered in its struggles over African American slavery and moved rapidly to isolate African Americans once they were freed. Chinese Americans were denied citizenship and the right to vote in California, a restraint that became federal law when Congress passed the 1882 Chinese Exclusion Act, making the Chinese "aliens ineligible for citizenship," and prohibiting nearly all Chinese immigration to the United States. Additional landholding restrictions were imposed on Japanese immigrants. By 1924, the Asian Exclusion Act barred all but a trickle of Asian immigration for permanent residence. The 1924 law remained in place until 1965 (Takaki 1993).

These legal constraints reflected views in the majority community and, from the founding until well into the twentieth century, United States historical records abound with racial stigmatizations against non-white groups. The definition of who counted as white was fluid, first excluding and later encompassing the Irish, southern and eastern Europeans and Jews. But the bias in favor of the United States as primarily a white nation was a constant, asserted by presidents, governors, editors, scholars, judges and countless ordinary citizens. Throughout this period, the white community made unremitting efforts, both legal and mob-driven, scientifically rationalized and emotional, to resist the dangers of racial intermarriage and consequent "mongrelization."

By the twentieth century, additional forms of segregation drew new divisions through the diverse communities that comprised the United States. As southern blacks began to move to northern cities in record numbers, these cities, through a combination of deliberate legal restraints, federal housing laws and personal intimidation, created huge neighborhoods that were exclusively African American in their composition. The South, where African Americans had typically lived side by side with whites, although subordinate to them, also moved toward new patterns of enforced residential segregation. As Massey and Denton (1993) observe in a powerful analysis of this construction of an "American Apartheid," the forms of twentieth-century segregation assigned to African Americans were different both in kind and in intensity from that experienced by other United States ethnic groups: "Even at the height of immigration from Europe, most Italians, Poles and Jews lived in neighborhoods where members of their own group did not predominate…In contrast, after the construction of the black ghetto the vast majority of blacks were forced to live in neighborhoods that were all black, yielding an extreme level of social isolation."

Higher education is uniquely heir to both these dimensions of American pluralism—the commitment to deliberation across difference as the genius of our democratic praxis and the continuing costs and consequences of historic patterns of selective discrimination compounded by racial segregation.

United States colleges and universities from the beginning acknowledged and embraced a special responsibility to ensure that the nation's leaders would be well prepared, intellectually and morally, for their responsibilities in a republic founded on reasoning. Traditions of free speech and unfettered inquiry were woven into the very fabric of the American research university. Intellectual diversity, dialogue and deliberation constitute distinctive strengths of American higher education.

Yet the color lines that divided United States communities for most of its history bounded college campuses as well. Into the 1960s, the nation's system of higher education was *de facto* almost completely racially segregated, basically either all-white or all-black with at best a 1 to 2 percent variation at some major institutions. Colleges founded to serve the African-American community were at least 99 percent black, and it was the rare majority college that was less than 97 percent white. Overall, minority participation in higher education was strikingly limited. As late as the fall of 1970, nearly 87 percent of college students in the United States were white. Nine percent were black and the combined total of Asian Americans, American Indians, and others was a mere 2.2 percent (Karen 1991). The curriculum at majority institutions was as "white" as the student body. Few courses and no core curricula challenged students to confront and explore the inherent contradictions between the nation's aspirations to human worth and dignity for all people and the persistence of its divisions and hierarchies.

From the mid-1960s on, however, leaders in the higher education community sought to alter these inheritances. Simultaneously inspired by the civil rights movement and alarmed by the 1960s ghetto rebellions and the aftermath of the Martin Luther King assassination, campus leaders made a new commitment to the expansion of both equality and opportunity and to the dismantling of systemic discrimination against any group. The women's movement which emerged at the end of the 1960s adopted much of the civil rights movement's language and vision of inclusion, adding a new dynamic of commitment and energy to campus leadership for access and equity.

These efforts, reinforced by dramatic alterations in immigration patterns since 1965, have begun to change the color of higher education. Today, nearly one quarter of those participating in higher education are persons of color. Campuses located in states experiencing high levels of immigration have seen diversity increase exponentially. Others, especially in the heartland states, have had to work much harder to change the racial and ethnic composition of their student bodies. But almost all campuses now see education of a diverse citizenry as integral to their missions of public leadership and service.

The curriculum is changing too. Notwithstanding the vigorously expressed doubts of many traditionally educated faculty members and public leaders, scholars have made extraordinary progress in recovering histories and legacies once deemed irrelevant to higher learning. Hundreds of colleges and universities are now seeking ways to change course content and requirements so that the curriculum includes the myriad forms of American diversity. Some of them are also asking students to study the very legacies of hierarchy and exclusion that used to leave most of humankind out of the curriculum.

This record of progress notwithstanding, success in extending participation in higher education across communities of color remains uneven. African Americans constitute 12.3 percent of the population but only 8.7 percent of college students and 5.7 percent of college graduates. Hispanics, who comprise 7.7 percent of the population, make up 4.9 percent of higher education students and 2.7 percent of graduates (Justiz, Wilson, and Björk 1994). Hispanic rates of participation and attainment have been declining rather than improving, and Mexican Americans in particular are severely underrepresented among those enrolled in higher education. American Indians have increased their participation at all levels of higher education but experience significant problems with retention. American citizens of Asian, Indian, Chinese, Filipino, Japanese, and Korean heritage have higher-than-average percentages of both high school and college graduation. But members of more recent Asian immigrant groups—for example, the Cambodians, Hmong, and Laotians—have educational profiles that resemble those of African Americans and American Indians (O'Brien 1995).

The perception of uneven participation is strengthened when we look at the question of where students of color have enrolled. Proportionately, their participation in community colleges is about the same as their participation in the population as a whole. But students of color constitute only 15 percent of enrollments in four year institutions, still a significant degree of underrepresentation.

Those who are unhappy with the magnitude and direction of change on campus and in society have attacked "diversity" as a spurious and even meaningless goal for higher education. It is important to remember that in higher education, the term "diversity" references a complex set of efforts to uproot the sources and legacies of a long history of societal hierarchy and educational apartheid. The academy is far from finished with this task.

United States colleges and universities are currently working on four distinct although interrelated dimensions of diversity, observes Daryl Smith of the Claremont Graduate School. "Representation" focuses on the absence of particular groups from the campus community and seeks ways to increase their numbers. "Campus Climate" recognizes the integral connections between institutional environment and educational attainment and seeks to change those aspects of campus climate that prove chilly for particular groups of students, whether members of designated groups, women, or the so-called "non-traditional" adults who are fast becoming a new majority in higher education. "Educational Mission" signals the realization that all students benefit from an education that fosters knowledge and competence for a multiracial, multiethnic, multiperspectival and gendered world. "Transformation" connects all the other dimensions of diversity in a fundamental reconsideration of the academy's organizing assumptions—societal, intellectual, educational and institutional (Smith 1995).

When the Association of American Colleges and Universities launched a national diversity initiative in 1993, our focus was on educational mission in its largest societal context: fostering social learning about United States diversity in relation to the nation's democratic aspiration and values. We titled this initiative American Commitments: Diversity, Democracy, and Liberal Learning, and began a broad effort both to describe the knowledge participants need in this diverse democracy and to identify effective ways of fostering this learning in goals for liberal education and the curriculum, in institutional life and campus ethos, and in the classroom practices that comprise teaching and learning.

Over time we have come to see that the dialogue in which we are engaged is indeed, as Smith's analysis suggests, transformational. Our focus on links between this nation's diversity and its democratic values has pointed the American Commitments initiative inexorably toward unresolved issues that cut across campus and society: issues of communities and community; issues of the terms and tensions that frame connection among members of a democracy who, historically, have not been equal.

Framing the question this way, those participating in the American Commitments initiative have grown increasingly uncomfortable with the individualistic assumptions that permeate public discussion of higher education. Traditionally, the academy has emphasized the benefits of higher learning—both intellectual and economic—to each individual learner. But diversity and democracy together press educators to address the communal dimensions and consequences of higher learning. By highlighting the social nexus in which all learning occurs, the linkage between diversity and democratic society challenges us to think more deeply about what individuals

Diversity and democracy together press educators to address the communal dimensions and consequences of higher learning.

learn from their experience of campus ethos—and how that learning in turn constrains or enriches the quality and vitality of American communities.

To guide what has become an exploration of both educational and societal vision, AAC&U formed a distinguished National Panel of scholars and academic leaders, all significant contributors to contemporary understandings of diversity in higher education and United States society. Members of the Panel began an extraordinary series of dialogues, in the group as a whole, in smaller subsets of the Panel, and in discussions with higher education colleagues at a series of working conferences throughout the country. To these discussions, Panel members brought their own diversities—societal, experiential, intellectual—not as suppressed background but as the context for everything they know and value and work for as leaders in higher education.

Panel members also came to the American Commitments initiative ready to learn from one another; transformational learning has been the great product of these two years of dialogue and deliberation. Frank Wong, the deeply respected Panel chair, stood at the moral center of the group's dialogue until his death in the spring of 1995. Wong modeled for everyone else a paradigmatic process of Madison's "yielding and accommodating" spirit as he sought to understand challenges to his initial assumptions, weaving them into his own contributions to the Panel's collectively developed view.

Panel members' analyses of connection and commitment in American society, deepened, complicated and reconfigured through two years of internal and public discussions of several draft reports, culminate in the publication of the report in this volume and four others in this series. Together, these National Panel reports provide a comprehensive examination of higher education's missions of leadership and service in a society that is diverse, divided by legacies of social and gender hierarchy, and yet still embarked on a historic wager that democratic dialogue across difference can lead all participants toward achievement of a just and equitable society.

HIGHER EDUCATION AS A TESTING GROUND FOR AMERICAN PLURALISM

In presenting these reports, we urge our colleagues to recognize that higher education faces a distinctive challenge and an extraordinary opportunity at what we take to be a pivotal moment in the development of United States pluralism. Educators often assume that higher education's efforts to become both diverse and inclusive simply reflect and parallel comparable commitments and progress in the wider society. In fact, however, societal movement towards inclusion is marked by both progress and striking regression.

Campuses, workplaces and the military have indeed become increasingly diverse and newly conscious that inclusion encompasses more than physical presence. But these institutional changes are occurring in the context of an increase, not a decrease, in the nation's racial and economic residential segregation.

This means that institutions which are meeting grounds for United States diversity assume the special responsibility of fostering capacities for and commitments to pluralism that are often not part of Americans' neighborhood experience. Attending a college or university may be the first experience of a notably diverse community many students have had. Participation in a community drawn from multiple cultures and experiences calls on an inclination to engage and learn across difference that many students have had no opportunity to achieve. It requires skills that have not been practiced—or valued.

Two-thirds of Americans now live in those combinations of cities and their surrounding suburbs that the Bureau of the Census designates as Standard Metropolitan Statistical Areas. But whether we look at the distribution of population in these SMSAs as a whole or at the composition of the urban core within them, the striking demographic trend is the intensification, not the diminution, of racial residential segregation. Even as the nation's laws have pressed Americans toward new forms of equality and connection, Americans have not only resisted residential integration but compounded and consolidated earlier twentieth-century patterns of residential segregation.

In the last quarter century, America's urban population has undergone the most dramatic racial recomposition in its entire history. Beginning in the 1970s, the urban core within each of ten major metropolitan areas experienced a precipitous decline in the proportion of its residents that are white. New York City dropped from 75 percent white in 1970 to 38 percent white in 1990. San Francisco has gone from 75 percent to 43 percent white while in Los Angeles, the drop is even greater, from 78 percent to 37 percent. There is a similar pattern for most major metropolitan areas in the nation. The whites who leave are moving to "vanilla" suburbs, communities where persons of color are strikingly underrepresented. Conversely, although persons of color are also moving to the suburbs, the suburbs too are now becoming dotted with segregated enclaves (Duster 1995).

As these changes are occurring, the intensity of racial segregation of the population within the city has been compounding. "In sixteen metropolitan areas that house one-third of the nation's black population," write Massey and Denton (1993), "racial separation is [now] so intense that it can only be described as hypersegregation." Especially for African Americans, patterns of racial residential separation hold at every income level, from the poorest to the most affluent. When they go home at night, blacks and whites in America go to entirely separate communities.

Other forms of societal division are also intensifying in the contemporary United States. As study after study reveals, patterns of economic inequal-

Our nation's campuses have become a highly visible stage on which the most fundamental questions about difference, equality, and community are being enacted.

ity—and the class-linked residential separations that mirror these patterns—are also compounding. The bottom three-fifths of the population are seeing their share of national income steadily decrease. The middle class feels increasingly pressed and increasingly dislocated. Statistically, it is shrinking. As the divide between well-off and extremely poor widens, the emergence of gated and often exclusive residential communities is a widely remarked social phenomenon.

In this era of increasing segregation and economic disequilibrium, the nation's long-standing legacies of racial antagonism are once again in play. Many see the efforts to reach out through affirmative action to bring disenfranchised minorities and women into institutions that excluded them as a crucial key to their own experience of economic "squeeze." Others, including many in communities of color, blame recently arrived immigrants, both legal and illegal, for closing off their own upward mobility. As in earlier periods when Americans felt economically threatened and therefore passed legislation hostile to immigrant groups, the country is again in the 1990s embarking on a new era of anti-immigrant feeling and policies.

In sum, as higher education moves forward to affirm and enact a commitment to equality, fairness, and inclusion, it does so in a context of increasing racial and class separations and antagonisms. The contemporary assault on affirmative action in higher education in California has shocked many educators for its astonishing presumption that in barely thirty years we have successfully resolved the nation's centuries of racial, ethnic, and gender contradictions. But this assault, certain to be imitated elsewhere, is symptomatic. Members of the academy who are leading diversity initiatives have been developing a knowledge of United States history that most of the country, educated on an abridged curriculum, does not possess. They are asserting the value of an engaged pluralism to which many Americans do not aspire.

HIGHER EDUCATION'S RESPONSIBILITY AND OPPORTUNITY

In its commitment to diversity, higher education assumes, therefore, both a distinctive responsibility and a precedent-setting challenge. While other institutions in the society are also fostering diversity, higher education is uniquely positioned, by its mission, values, and dedication to learning, to foster and nourish the habits of heart and mind that Americans need to make diversity work in daily life. We have an opportunity to help our campuses experience engagement across difference as a value and a public good.

Our nation's campuses have become a highly visible stage on which the most fundamental questions about difference, equality, and community are being enacted. To this effort, filled with promise and fraught with difficulty, the academy brings indispensable resources: its commitments to the advancement of knowledge and its traditions of dialogue and deliberation across difference as keys to the increase of insight and understanding.

This report and the others in this series describe ways that higher education can respond to the challenge of this pivotal moment in the American drama. Formed as we are by the academy's strong traditions of intellectual and social pluralism, higher education faces a rich opportunity to put its own commitments to knowledge at the nation's service.

We urge our colleagues to engage the reflections on the American past and future offered in these pages and draw from them a heightened sense of responsibility and possibility for our nation's brave and risky wager that dialogue across diversity can, in the end, nourish wisdom, understanding and the increase of justice.

CAROL SCHNEIDER
Director, The American Commitments Initiative

SYNOPSIS

Over the past hundred years, the academy has remade its conceptions of knowledge and revised repeatedly the content and variety of its curricula. None of these transformations were simply reactive to external demands, but neither were they independent of societal context. As Frederick Rudolph writes, "Curricular history is American history and therefore carries the burden of revealing the central purposes and driving directions of American Society."

Higher education's current debate about foregrounding diversity in the curriculum is part of the academy's continuing engagement with the wider society and with fundamental societal questions. Our dialogues about diversity are difficult because they ultimately raise questions about the foundations, justice, decency, and creativity of United States democracy. These in turn become questions about our capacity to imagine and build a future in which all who live here have a valued role and an equal stake. The curriculum becomes a ground on which Americans probe the relations between differing memories of history and the forms of our future connections.

Higher education's deliberation about forms of human difference and their inclusion in the curriculum are not, as some charge, a politicization of knowledge. The curriculum always expresses judgments about issues that are important to society and therefore important as subjects of study. In debating the significance of societal diversity for the curriculum, the academy is doing what it is charged to do: explore fundamental questions and submit both previous assumptions and established traditions to rigorous examination.

KNOWLEDGE
AND THE
CURRICULUM

Over a two-year period, AAC&U's American Commitments initiative has sponsored dozens of dialogues across the country about higher education's role in preparing graduates for the cultural and democratic pluralism of this society. Participants in these dialogues repeatedly made the following points:

FRAMING
THE QUESTION

- Those who live in this country have had markedly disparate experiences—both positive and negative—of United States societal diversity and of this country's willingness to recognize all its peoples.

- Americans therefore hold radically differing views—both optimistic and profoundly pessimistic—about this country's effective commitment to meaningful equality.

- The call for diversity in the curriculum challenges Americans to recognize, value, and learn from this country's extraordinarily heterogeneous cultures, communities, and perspectives. It is a call to recognize and address the persistence of unequal power and dramatically unequal access to resources and opportunity in the United States.

The inclination to begin our diversity dialogue with "common values" invites a premature and thus exclusionary rush to closure.

- Many educated Americans have a learned preference to emphasize what "we" hold in common. This preference, while well-intentioned, overlooks the issues of unequal power and marginalization that are central to the contemporary diversity dialogue. It also undervalues the contribution that diverse communities can make to the search for renewal and community in American life.

- The inclination to begin with "common values" therefore invites a premature and thus exclusionary rush to closure. The difficult dialogues of diversity require from the outset respectful attention to one another's stories and viewpoints. Before Americans can address the problems of division, recognition, and meaningful opportunity that confront our communities, we need to hear and learn from the perspectives of those most acutely affected.

DIVERSITY, DEMOCRACY, AND THE COLLEGE CURRICULUM

Higher education has a central role to play in preparing students for the complexity and diversity of their society. But we need a much richer conception than most campuses hold of the curriculum basic to this preparation. In this richer conception, education for democratic pluralism is just as important as education in cultural pluralism.

Education for United States democratic and cultural pluralism is not the same task, we emphasize, as the education for global knowledge and interconnection in which so many institutions are currently engaged. Students require both global knowledge and domestic knowledge. Colleges and universities shortchange their students when they view courses on world cultures and United States diversity as interchangeable, or leave attention to United States diversity optional and elective. Education for participation in United States cultural and democratic pluralism is preparation for citizenship and leadership. It deserves its own time and space in the curriculum.

The American Commitments National Panel has framed four recommendations about education for citizenship in a diverse democracy. The recommendations are designed to:

- create a level playing field on which everyone holds an equal stake in explorations of societal experiences, identities, and aspirations;

- impart knowledge of the diverse cultures, communities, and histories that comprise United States society;

- connect these diversities to a continuing engagement with democratic ideas and aspirations;

- provide experiential as well as formal knowledge of these topics; and

- prepare students for a world in which unitary agreement does not now exist and is not likely ever to exist.

Toward those goals, the panel recommends four kinds of courses and experiences, as follows:

1. EXPERIENCE, IDENTITY, AND ASPIRATION: The study of one's own particular inherited and constructed traditions, identity communities, and significant questions, in their complexity.

2. UNITED STATES PLURALISM AND THE PURSUITS OF JUSTICE: An extended and comparative exploration of diverse peoples in this society, with significant attention to their differing experiences of United States democracy and the pursuits—sometimes successful, sometimes frustrated—of equal opportunity.

3. EXPERIENCES IN JUSTICE SEEKING: Encounters with systemic constraints on the development of human potential in the United States and experiences in community-based efforts to articulate principles of justice, expand opportunity, and redress inequities.

4. MULTIPLICITY AND RELATIONAL PLURALISM IN MAJORS, CONCENTRATIONS, AND PROGRAMS: Extensive participation in forms of learning that foster sustained exploration of and deliberation about contested issues important in particular communities of inquiry and practice.

Taken together, these complementary forms of learning—personal, societal, participatory, and dialogical—constitute an appropriate college curriculum for effective citizenship in a diverse democracy. In calling for this curriculum, we are asserting that students must learn, in every part of their educational experience, to live creatively with the multiplicity, ambiguity, and irreducible differences that are the defining conditions of the contemporary world.

INTRODUCTION

This report on United States diversity and the college curriculum builds on a foundational principle which might be thought self-evident, but which, because it is often vigorously contested, requires discussion, not simply assertion.

The curriculum refracts the society of which it is a part. It both re-presents and influences the larger community. Societal developments—transformations in political and material relations, alterations in domestic and international affairs, changes in consciousness—all prompt new needs and new uses for knowledge. Our expectations of higher learning and the curricula designed to address those expectations must evolve as society evolves. The integrity and vitality of our curricula depend on higher education's thoughtful responsiveness to these societal changes.

Over the past hundred years, the academy has remade its conceptions of knowledge; reconceived the scope and forms of its inquiry; revised repeatedly the content and variety of its curricula; accomplished revolutionary changes in the size, composition, and ethos of its educational communities. None of these transformations was simply reactive to external demands, but neither were they independent of societal context. As Frederick Rudolph (1977) writes, "Curricular history is American history and therefore carries the burden of revealing the central purposes and driving directions of American society."

To say that the academy does and should respond to societal developments is not to abandon higher education's critical function, its central and powerful traditions of intellectual leadership and social critique. It is rather to say that the academy stakes its claims to both leadership and service on a continuous and searching engagement with questions that are not "academic" and issues whose outcome will make a real difference to some aspect of our lives.

In meeting these expectations for leadership and service, both the faculty and the curriculum must be integrally involved with the larger society's great questions, central institutions, inventive practices, contested expectations, unmet needs. Those who graduate from American colleges and universities should be able to see clear connections between what they have learned in college and the societal contexts in which their learning will make a difference. These connections and students' understanding of them are the fulfillment of what we call liberal education.

The academy stakes its claims to both leadership and service on a continuous and searching engagement with questions that are not "academic" and issues whose outcome will make a real difference to some aspect of our lives.

The subject of this report—recommendations for the teaching of United States diversity in the curriculum—is part of the academy's central engagement with wider communities and fundamental societal questions. The complex issues that comprise today's difficult diversity dialogues are questions about the foundations, justice, decency, and creativity of United States society. They are questions about the influences of our pasts on possible futures. They are questions, at root, about our capacity to imagine and build a democratic future in which all who live here, whatever their religion, gender, ethnicity, class, ability, or origin in another culture, have a valued role and an equal stake.

CHAPTER ONE

HIGHER EDUCATION AND UNITED STATES DIVERSITY

I n the past two years, the American Commitments initiative held dozens of dialogues across the country about higher education's role in the future of this diverse democracy. A telling moment at one of these forums helps crystallize the issues at stake in these discussions. The exchange occurred at an American Commitments leadership institute. A plenary speaker had just concluded remarks about democracy and diversity and was taking questions and comments from the audience. The first person to respond was a woman of American Indian heritage who stood up in the back of the room and said, quietly and simply, "For me, democracy is a lie."

The speaker did not quite catch her words and asked her to repeat them. At once, several people tried to help with a translation. "She said, 'Democracy is alive,'" they all explained in unison. Then someone who knew the woman and her views added her own voice in irritation. "No, democracy is a *lie*," she repeated urgently. And then, for a moment, all around the room, as over one hundred people sought to get it right, some people were saying, "Democracy is a lie" while still others were insisting, "No, it's alive."

These few moments of missed communication offer a framing encounter in which different perceptions of United States reality came jaggedly into confrontation with one another. Some members of this society do indeed believe that democracy is only as good as its practice. And the practice as they experience it shows them plainly that this society's democratic claims—its claims to provide equal recognition, participation, and dignity for all members of our communities—are not true.

Others, both on campus and off, take democracy for granted as part of the distinctive goodness of United States society. There is no connection at all in their minds between the concept of democracy and the word "lie." And still others—including those involved in AAC&U's American Commitments initiative—believe democracy can be alive only as long as we are attending to the full meaning of democratic aspiration, as long as we are forcing the question: What would it mean for democracy to be truly alive for every person in this society?

What is especially significant in this story is the realization that people who had come to a conference on diversity were not able to hear one another. Despite their shared interest in the topic and their openness to an

It is in the juxtapositions of different truths that our dialogues about diversity—and our curricula—must begin.

Certain differences correlate with differential power in United States society. Difference cannot therefore be simply ignored.

extended exploration, different participants' assumptions were so disparate that language did not, at first, communicate. And even when the language was explained, when it was clear that the American Indian woman firmly believed democratic claims of equal participation and inclusion to be a lie, many in the room were genuinely taken aback that she would say such a thing.

Participants in the larger society, as in this forum, hold different memories of United States pluralism. They hold different understandings of such basic terms in our civic lexicon as justice and equality. Out of these differences, they have forged competing truths. That reality is the central challenge we face as educators.

It is in these juxtapositions of different truths that our dialogues about diversity—and our curricula—must begin. Human experiences in this country have not been all alike or all benign. Those marked out by racial, ethnic, economic, or other forms of marginalized diversity have not had the same kinds of experience with United States society as those who identify with and are readily accepted by the dominant European-American cultural and socioeconomic communities. Many people of color, many in our economically divided cities, and many white Americans living a marginal economic existence all too readily understand the assertion, "The claim of equality does not include me."

Yet those who live here want, with few exceptions, to participate in the life and possibility of United States society. We want more than the elucidation of our differences. Implicitly, if not always explicitly, most want this country to live up to the implied promises of its democratic heritage: to provide in experience as well as principle equal dignity, communality, opportunity, and justice. We continue to grapple as a people both with the implications of that wish and with the complexities and pain of our mingled histories.

The resurgent attention to race, to select just one strand in our complicated diversity matrix, confronts us with questions about both the past and the future. What can and will we do about the embedded inequities and injustices, economic and interpersonal, that are attached to racial constructs and racial stigmatizations in United States history and society? On what terms do persons with different relations to our racial history move forward together? What does a commitment to justice entail? Does working to redress injustice mean working to remove the practical significance of difference? Or are we committing ourselves to recognize the realities of difference and learn to value their potential complementaries? Or do we do both, and what would that mean?

If race presses us back to a complicated struggle with past and future, so too do gender, class, ethnicity, religion, sexual identity, and other sources of human connection and human difference. For a long time, the dominant culture treated these particularities, separate and intersecting, as though they were only epiphenomena in the American societal economy. And yet, as many of us acknowledge, these dimensions of identity are fundamental sources of voice, meaning, and connection in our society.

At the same time, as every one of us also knows, these particularities that shape human identity have mattered powerfully in United States history—and matter to this moment—in distinguishing between those more likely to remain perpetually on the margins and those with greater access to social resources and power. Certain differences correlate with differential power in United States society. Difference cannot therefore be simply ignored.

CHAPTER TWO
AMERICAN PLURALISM
AND THE CURRICULUM

Many have called our present societal debate a national dialogue about multiculturalism. The truth is that these debates raise questions that extend well beyond the exploration of multiple cultures, if we understand culture to mean social constructions of moral order, the shared meanings that inform how communities live. This debate over difference is about unequal power and persistent exclusions as much as it is about culture. Taken in its fullest terms, it ought to force a new and more searching engagement with issues of justice, equity, mutual recognition, economic empowerment, democratic aspiration, and moral involvement.

These issues and the debates about them belong in the college curriculum. For those who live in this society, they comprise an essential, not an elective, curriculum.

Our campuses must help our diverse communities engage fundamental questions of knowledge, principle, and human capacity:

- What must we know and understand about the multiplicity of groups and people that have been unequally acknowledged and included in our nation?

- How are we to understand the disparity between democratic aspirations and the persistence of unequal participation in United States society? How do we address them?

- What relational principles can we envision in this phase of our evolution as a democracy to guide us in forging new civic covenants and more just relations among both individuals and groups?

- What capacities must we develop to negotiate disparate and multiple commitments and communities, inherited and adopted, and to encounter diversity—in the society and in ourselves—as a resource rather than a threat?

- What are the crucial distinctions between merely acknowledging difference and learning to take grounded stands in the face of difference? Recognizing multiplicity as a given in our societal situation, how do we foster the development of each person's sense of self, voice, particularity, and moral vision?

Our present societal debate over difference is about unequal power and persistent exclusions as much as it is about culture.

As educators we must address these basic challenges for American pluralism across the curriculum—in the classroom, in the co-curriculum, in the intersections between campus and community. Our students will need to grapple with a country that is not only diverse but divided. To do this, they must come to understand and respect peoples and ways of life that have been hidden from them. They must develop the willingness to engage the range of perspectives that mingle side by side in United States communities. They must cross cultural borders and forge relationships with parts of this society—even parts of their own cities—that they have never entered and would not now be comfortable entering.

The many demands for voice, recognition, and full participation that reverberate through both nation and campus appeal implicitly and sometimes explicitly to this country's heritage of democratic aspiration, achievement, and failure. Where are our students learning to comprehend the intricacies of that heritage? How will they develop the complex set of capacities and knowledge and dispositions necessary to navigate our competing truths? Neither our contemporary national political discourse nor instruction in the schools is providing a foundation upon which effective citizenship and leadership in a diverse democracy may be built.

The academy's current deliberation about forms of human difference and their implications for liberal education are not then, as some have charged, a crude politicization of knowledge and the curriculum. The curriculum always expresses judgments about societal deliberation important in a given time and place. It foregrounds particular questions at particular moments in time. These questions, of necessity, evolve.

What we are experiencing now in the academy and the larger society is the disruption of earlier judgments about the societal knowledge, values, and questions that ought to be reflected in higher education. Or, in other words, the broad and complex debate about a nexus of issues we term multiculturalism, diversity, or difference is part of the disturbance, disruption, and creative ferment that inevitably occur when the academy, in dialogue with the wider community, turns its attention to fundamental questions and, in so doing, challenges both previous assumptions and customary codes. When the academy practices its espoused values, submitting its traditions to the disciplines of rigorous, extensive, and multifocal interrogation, debate is always unleashed.

Our students must cross cultural borders and forge relationships with parts of this society—even parts of their own cities—that they have never entered and would not now be comfortable entering.

FRAMING THE QUESTION

As its title suggests, this national initiative called American Commitments: Diversity, Democracy, and Liberal Learning frames diversity questions as a searching exploration of United States justice, histories, equity, mutual recognition across racial and ethnic boundaries, economic empowerment, democratic aspiration, and moral engagement.

Many in the academy have raised questions about this framing in one or another of the forums sponsored by the American Commitments initiative. Some point to the importance of cultural knowledge and sensitivity as a job skill. Those who work will do so in intercultural settings that place a premium on high-performance collaborative workgroups. Surely, these colleagues urge, the needs of the workplace offer the most persuasive argument for including diversity in the curriculum. Almost everyone recognizes the economic imperative for enlarging Americans' cultural knowledge and understanding. Economic imperatives can open both doors and minds.

Others have queried the American Commitments focus on United States diversity. American students need to know about world cultures, not just about United States pluralism, these colleagues urge. Why not cast a broader net?

Nothing we say in this report opposes these arguments for opening the contemporary college curriculum to new voices, new perspectives, and previously excluded histories. Preparation for the world of work is important, and competence in working with diverse peoples is an important part of that preparation. Similarly, all students need to study world cultures and global interdependencies. An ever larger share of the curriculum is being and should be devoted to world studies. Colleges and universities are already working on both these topics and will continue to do so.

We focus in these American Commitments reports, however, on domestic issues that must be addressed as students prepare to assume responsibility for this extraordinarily diverse society. Navigating the issues of justice, equity, power, and opportunity in this complex society is not simply a matter of greater cultural sensitivity in the workplace, even though the workplace is certainly a central laboratory for American pluralism. Nor are students sufficiently educated for United States diversity when they have met a graduation requirement that directs them to take one or more courses on a non-Anglo American culture or to develop facility in "reading" the artifacts of an unfamiliar world culture. While such expectations are essential parts of a contemporary education, they are insufficient preparation for the unfinished work of this diverse democracy. It is quite possible to learn a great deal about Chinese art or the Russian economy or about great African kingdoms and still be surprised that many in the United States doubt the integrity of this country's justice. One can know a great deal about cultures around the world and very little about the tangled expectations that attach to traditions of American democratic aspiration.

It is for these reasons that the American Commitments initiative focuses on American diversity in the context of United States histories, democratic values, and possibilities. The challenges that confront this democracy are fundamental. Americans already take for granted a state of affairs in

What we are experiencing now in the academy and the larger society is the disruption of earlier judgments about the societal knowledge, values, and questions that ought to be reflected in higher education.

which many of us never enter entire communities because of their and our racial, ethnic, and/or economic composition. Many citizens are routinely denied equal rights because of their sexual orientation. The economic divisions in this country are widening, not narrowing. The contemporary debates about immigration and welfare both show that most citizens know far too little about either the history or the contemporary complexity of these vintage American topics. Studies routinely report how differently blacks and whites perceive the same issues in the United States. At the same time, persons of Latino or Asian or Arab American heritage are constantly frustrated that black-white issues so frame racial analysis in the United States that the particularities of other ethnic and racial configurations are lost.

Nearly 60 percent of high school graduates now spend at least some period of time in college. If they devote at least a part of this time to an education that better prepares them to grasp the complexity and multiplicity of the society in which they live, we as a people will gain a mobilization of civic intelligence, knowledge, and practice for our communities that this country sorely needs.

LIBERAL EDUCATION AND THE LIMITS OF UNIVERSALISM

If there is a single theme that runs through contemporary debates about American pluralism, it is the insistent assertion from educated people, "We need to focus on what we have in common. Our commonalities are more important than our differences."

Given this widespread wish to emphasize what "we" presumably share, the academy has been divided not just by questions of how to more fully reflect the diversity of our society in the curriculum, but, more fundamentally, about whether it is even desirable to do so. Why are so many, including notable scholars and thoughtful leaders, vocally alarmed that in mapping issues of United States cultural and societal difference into the college curriculum, we will lose something fundamental in the developed traditions of American liberal education and, therefore, in our societal community?

One key to this puzzle lies in the particular assumptions about learning and society that, until very recently, were woven, almost unquestioned, into the fabric of liberal education in the academy. As we have seen, the curriculum always mediates conceptions of knowledge and society. American traditions of liberal education have been closely tied to the core values of liberal democracies and especially to the core values of our own liberal democracy. And liberalism as an ethos, as historian Joyce Appleby (1992) has forcefully documented, is distinctive, indeed remarkable, for its determination to align itself with universal, meta-historical processes and principles.

These universalizing tendencies of western liberalism are firmly rooted in its successful struggles against the entrenched and oppressive accretions of history. When liberalism first emerged as a transformative force in the eighteenth century, its proponents were loathe to justify reforms they sought as good merely for a particular time and place. Instead, they deliberately made the universal both their warrant and their espoused goal.

Accordingly, liberal spokesmen aligned themselves early on with nature, reason, and eventually science, each seen as governed by orderly principles susceptible to discovery and eventual management by the developed capacities of the human mind.

Western democracies depend still on universal claims and premises—human nature, natural rights, the principles of free societies, the laws of markets—to buttress the case for their societal aspirations, central commitments, and preferred practices. At its best, this universalism is part of their appeal: liberal societies assert principles of human dignity and natural rights for all persons and not simply for their own citizens.

But as a set of intellectual constructs, western universalism has also been flawed and partial, built on premises that were both myopic and exclusionary. Western universalism, with its highly selective interpretations of what "we" hold in common as human beings, has therefore alienated and frustrated many of those—women, religious and ethnic minorities, persons of color—to whom its principles theoretically apply but who had, in fact, little or no part in their historical articulation and whose experience has often been the opposite of the noble ideals embedded in these very universals.

Through this century, liberal education in the United States has mirrored these features—positive and negative—of Enlightenment thought. Its fundamental conceptions, values, and structures have reflected and supported the universalistic, transhistorical premises and self-understandings of this broad and influential tradition in liberal societies. Liberal education has thus predisposed educated people toward a preference for identifying the common or universal themes in human experience, which means, in practice, discomfort with approaches that reveal basic, perhaps unassimilable, differences.

Philosopher John Searle (1993) usefully shows us how profoundly the premises and self-understandings of western liberalism have shaped the academy's goals for liberal education. The western tradition, he notes approvingly, is characterized by

> a peculiar combination of what one might call extreme universalism and extreme individualism....This tends to be tacit and is seldom made explicit. The idea is that the most precious thing in the universe is the human individual, but that the human individual is precious as part of the universal human civilization....[O]ne achieves one's maximum intellectual *individual* potential by coming to see oneself as part of a *universal* human species with a universal human culture.

Liberal education has predisposed educated people toward a preference for identifying the common or universal themes in human experience, which means, in practice, discomfort with approaches that reveal basic, perhaps unassimilable, differences.

11

It is because the ethos of liberal education has been integrally connected to images of a transcendent human society, rather than to the issues of any particular societies, that the "multicultural" debate is so disorienting.

What follows from this aspiration is a view of education as liberatory from the contingencies of time and place and liberatory too from one's original cultural attachments and/or original community. Education viewed in these terms aims at helping the student overcome the parochialism of personal experience. It seeks to make students citizens of the world, makers of a universal community.

Searle puts it this way:

> One of the things we are trying to do is to enable our students to overcome the mediocrity, provincialism, or other limitations of whatever background from which they may have come. The idea is that your life is likely to be in large measure a product of a lot of historical accidents: the town you were born in, the community you grew up in….One of the aims of a liberal education is to liberate our students from…[these] contingencies.…[We offer] what one might call an invitation to transcendence.

AAC&U's own classic statement about liberal education, *Integrity in the College Curriculum* (1985), offers another version of this same aspiration:

> Any subject, if presented liberally, will take students into a world beyond themselves, so that they may return and know themselves better. All study is intended to break down the narrow certainties and provincial vision with which we are born.

These formulations for liberal education are familiar and comfortable to many of us. Because many readers of this report have probably expressed their own educational values in much these terms, we need to stop and pause over what they say and what is omitted.

What we find in this understanding of liberal education is a robust conception of liberated selves, of transcendent individuals who, by overcoming their original ties, come to "know themselves better."

What we do not find in this model are conceptions of particular cultures, distinctive cultural traditions, or situated communal commitments and obligations. There is no sense of the individual's dependence on or obligations to specific communities. Nor is there a sense of the importance, both to the individual and to the society, of mediating communities that provide meaning and support for individuals and families. Lacking as well is any sense of the complex interconnections among such communities, of the borderland areas in which individuals negotiate multiple and often competing obligations and commitments.

This juxtaposition of individual and humanity as the polar axes of experience precludes articulation of conceptual frameworks that might help us deal productively with a world comprised of myriad, intersecting, smaller communities. Knowledge, in this tradition, means finding the self, but leaving the community of origin. It means finding overarching principles, but detaching from entangling particularities; embracing civilization, but overcoming ethnic inheritance. There is no hint in this model for liberal education that particular cultural or religious inheritances might be precious or enriching. There is nothing to suggest that the communal traditions of our diverse cultures might provide a valuable correction to an enlightenment heritage in which traditions of individualistic autonomy are significantly over-developed. There is no recognition that moral vision and capacity develop more readily in relation to a known community than to an imagined but abstract "human community."

In these inherited conceptions of liberal education, it is quite possible to think of oneself as a citizen of the world without learning much about one's own formative cultural traditions, whether secular or religious or both. The great majority of our college graduates have indeed, for many years, been welcomed into the world of educated United States citizens without knowing anything at all about the dozens of particular cultural traditions and historical memories that dwell together, tensely, uneasily, in our sprawling federation of states, cities, suburbs, and borderlands.

It is, in short, because the ethos of liberal education has been integrally connected to images of a transcendent human society, rather than to the issues of any particular societies, that the "multicultural" debate is so disorienting both to the academy and to those educated to leadership within our academies. Trained to believe that what is common or universal is by definition superior, many Americans find the new attention to diversity, difference, and cultural multiplicity disruptive. Well educated in the academy as it has been, they find themselves ill-equipped at the turn of the twenty-first century to recognize difference and the engagement of difference as sources of renewal and vitality in our educational and associational communities.

CHAPTER THREE
ENLIGHTENMENT ETHOS AND PREVALENT MODELS FOR GENERAL EDUCATION

Since the disappearance of the nineteenth-century classical common curriculum from American colleges and universities, there have been two dominant curricular strategies for preparing students for their roles as participants in the larger society. The influence of this universalistic ethos is fully evident in both of them:

- the tradition of the *dedicated course* or course sequence, variously titled Western Civilization, Human Heritage, or simply, Humanities; and

- a focus on *"ways of knowing,"* or the cultivation, primarily through study in the disciplines, of rational and critical capacities thought fundamental to a free society.

Each of these two traditions has privileged a version of the universal over the particular, the transhistorical over the contextual. Each has the practical effect of discouraging, in practice if not in explicit precept, attention to issues of identity, intersecting communities, voice, power, and agency within the specific society—the United States—that is our immediate responsibility as citizens.

Western Civilization/Human Heritage

The dedicated course model, which first emerged after World War I as the United States began to assert its world responsibilities, featured studies of Western Civilization/Human Heritage organized around a narrative of the West's discovery, cultivation, and expansion of the principles of societal liberty. Typical topics in such courses include the affirmation of human rationality and capacity for self-government (the Greeks); the rule of law (the Romans); the centrality of the individual (Christianity and the Renaissance); religious diversity and the concept of tolerance (post-Reformation Europe); the emergence of constitutional government and parliaments (early modern Europe); and the rise of science, liberal democracies, and market economies (the Enlightenment, the United States, and modern Europe).

Educational discussions of critical thinking, problem solving, or communication typically treat these capacities almost as architectonic functions of the mind—not as situated, societally specific, inevitably partial approaches.

These twin traditions of liberal education have had the practical effect of drawing the attention of educated persons away from the particular challenges, the continuing commitments of the society— the United States—for which they are most locally, most immediately responsible.

Distinctively, these Western Civilization/Human Heritage courses—first devised after World War I to prepare students for their responsibilities as citizens—traditionally touched lightly or not at all on American history. Thus students prepared for leadership in their own society by aligning themselves simultaneously with the "West" as the most important part of the world and with the "West" construed as universal societal principles which were both its distinctive achievement and its continuing responsibility. In this context, Western Civilization/Human Heritage courses presented democratic ideas and values as the discovery of universal principles rather than the situated, still-evolving, deeply flawed, and actively contested practices of specific societies in specific times and places.

Ways of Knowing/Critical Thinking

Whether or not they offered such dedicated courses on Western Civilization and Human Heritage, colleges and universities have routinely argued throughout this century that the second curricular strategy, the cultivation of critical and analytical capacities, is equally or even more important as part of students' preparation for the public sphere. Over the last two decades, especially, as nearly every college and university in the country reviewed its general education requirements, virtually all have reaffirmed "ways of knowing" and critical capacities as the centerpiece of liberal education and the academy's most valuable contribution to the larger society.

If we review classic statements of the critical capacities and ways of knowing, we find that these educational goals are also typically decontextualized, that is, detached from connection with any particular questions that might be asked about the past, present, and future of United States society. Educational discussions of critical thinking, problem solving, or communication typically treat these capacities almost as architectonic functions of the mind. Rarely are they addressed as situated, societally specific, necessarily partial approaches, linked to the values and needs of this society but not necessarily universal in all societies.

Consider, again, *Integrity in the College Curriculum*, AAC&U's own 1985 "minimum required curriculum" for liberal learning, which has been widely cited in campus reviews of general education or graduate requirements.

Integrity recommends cultivation of "historical consciousness," but not the study of any particular history; "inquiry, abstract logical thinking, critical analysis," but no particular critical questions facing contemporary society; values inquiry, but no values questions that have overriding importance to our communities. *Integrity*'s "minimum required curriculum," like Harvard's influential "core curriculum" before it, is deliberately content-flexible. Both feature intellectual capacities and habits of mind or, as *Integrity* terms it, "methods and processes"; both avow that these capacities can be developed through any number of different courses and curricula.

What matters in this widely shared contemporary conception of liberal learning as preparation for citizenship is the cultivation of reason and judgment. The academy develops the individual's mind. It does not necessarily insist that the individual develop deep knowledge of the principles and values espoused in democratic societies, nor of the histories that reveal the meanings, complexities and failures of those principles. Nor does it nurture the capacities and dispositions important to the practice of participatory democracy.

General education requirements on many campuses typically mix parts of both these dominant curricular models. Students may take required courses that map humanistic representations of the contemporary world and its tributaries; they are expected also to develop, across the whole of their studies, an understanding of different ways of knowing, the disposition to question givens, and the capacity to develop well-reasoned arguments.

Taken together, these curricular strategies—to the uneven extent that they are actually effective—have imparted both knowledge of Western values and institutions *and* the intellectual habits associated with Western rationalism.

All of this is so familiar, so deeply embedded in the culture of the academy, that the reader may wonder why it should be described. What does it have to do with diversity? Are these descriptions not the virtues of a liberal education, rather than its failings?

Our position is that these twin traditions of liberal education, inscripted in the graduation requirements of almost all our colleges and universities, *have had the practical effect of drawing the attention of educated persons away from the particular challenges, the continuing commitments of the society—the United States—for which they are most locally, most immediately responsible.*

This effect is inherent in the vision. As Searle reminds us, those of us who value liberal education have long sought to draw students away from their original cultures and communities into a larger, more encompassing society: the community of the intellect, the human community. Such a belief leads to the study of humankind, but not of one's neighbors; of ancient philosophers, but not of one's own family, identity, values, or commitments; of scientific principles and methods, but not of the effects of particular scientific developments on one's own communities.

These prevalent models for general liberal education, whether taken separately or mingled together, provide an education for public life that leaves the typical college graduate largely oblivious to the structures and inheritances of United States diversity and pluralism, ignorant of the troubled history of this particular democracy, unfamiliar with its democratic traditions and contested principles except in the most superficial terms, and absolutely unprepared to come to terms either with the cultural richness or with the real and embedded problems that confront this society.

Cornel West (1994) calls our attention to what is at stake in our rethinking of the received assumptions that connect liberal learning with universalist ideals and aspirations.

When one looks at the decolonization of the third world, what does one see? Psychic and physical violence: deep scars, bruises, wounds, tears, visceral levels of scars and bruises and wounds and tears. [Multiculturalism] is a critique of the discourse of universality, impartiality, objectivity, so often a cloak for the justification, the legitimation of those scars and bruises and tears.

As we survey the profound issues that confront American society: issues of cultural diversity and cultural, racial, ethnic and other inequities; issues of justice, mutual recognition, economic empowerment; issues of democratic principle and aspiration, we must ask whether our society can afford an unmodified perpetuation of these embedded traditions of educational "transcendence." The absence of any broad curricular discourse about these fundamental issues has contributed to the highly emotional and yet intellectually impoverished state of our national public discourse about diversity.

THE SHIFT FROM WESTERN "CIV" TO WORLD CULTURES

These dominant models for contemporary liberal general education are not, of course, static. Many colleges and universities, as AAC&U already has reported in a recent study (Schmitz 1992), are actively at work transforming the old Western Civilization/Human Heritage curricula in general education. They are doing so, many of them report, to prepare their students more adequately for a world characterized by cultural diversity and multiplicity.

The new general education core courses being developed across the country are more likely to feature comparative "cultures" than the study of "civilization"; they almost always include world content rather than an exclusive focus on the West. Stanford's much-debated addition of some "world" texts to a set of western readings is actually among the more modest of widespread contemporary efforts to remap older models for Western Civilization and Humanities courses. Many institutions have gone much further.

On some campuses, new required core courses deliberately contrast "West" and "World"; others focus on the diversity rather than the unities of the West; still others have recast their organizing principles to focus primarily on the World, with specific representations of Western epochs and/or cultures subordinate to an overarching emphasis on world interdependence or on comparative contrasts between different world societies. These new courses seek to train students in examining these traditions and cultures by fully engaging their histories, conflicts, and values.

These are promising curricular developments. The American Commitments initiative is strongly in favor of continued experimentation with ways of bringing comparative world cultures and perspectives into the core curriculum.

But these new curricular designs, valuable though they may be in themselves, also perpetuate the older tradition of transcending—that is, by default, ignoring—the history and problems that ought to engage us as participants in the United States. Moreover, soberingly, most of these newer models characteristically do not address, either historically or comparatively, the emergence of democratic ideas, institutions, and contestations. While the new models prepare students to understand better such topics as cultural difference, cultural encounter, and cultural translation, they frequently do not provide grounding in either the multiple cultural legacies or the equity issues that confound the United States in this stage of its development. Nor do they provide anything like a searching exploration of the democratic principles and aspirations to which participants appeal in discussions of basic societal questions.

CHAPTER FOUR
DIVERSITY, DEMOCRACY, AND THE COLLEGE CURRICULUM

The challenges that face the United States as we move into the next stage of our history call for a new educational ethos in our colleges and universities. This ethos must take diversity—in all its multiple forms—as a given and democratic communality as a framework in which all Americans search for answers to questions that confront this society. In the sections that follow, we propose educational principles and curricular practices that comprise a new direction for contemporary liberal education. The core conviction that guides these proposals is a belief that we must make a renewed commitment to produce graduates who bring self-knowledge, principle, intentionality and experience to the making of a diverse democracy.

- Because one's own particular inheritances and experiences form an interpretive framework both for the construction of identity and for all further learning, all students should be encouraged to study these inheritances and to become conversant with and conscious of the images, symbols, stories, and vocabularies that comprise their own experience of cultural connections and particularities.

  This is not an agenda for cultural minorities. *All* students should explore the distinctive roots and sources of their particular assumptions about value, meaning, significance, and obligation so that all engage these issues of cultural identity and interconnection on an equal footing. Nor should such studies be unitary. Students should be encouraged to recognize the complex and intersecting strands of inheritance and identification that make them who they are. Few Americans are defined by a singular cultural tradition.

- Because our graduates will be part of a society that depends on engagement across difference, they need studies and experiences that enable them to become fluent in one another's vocabularies and histories and to discover value in other ways of conceiving the world.

We must find ways of helping students learn through engagement with difference, including conflictual, uncongenial forms of human dissent, so that they may construct, together, new affirmations of social reciprocity and ethical obligations.

- Because our students are part of a society which is pluralistic and multi-cultural, they need courses that introduce them to comparative, relational studies. No undergraduate can be expected to know well all the world traditions that now mingle together in United States communities. But each can be expected to know several major United States cultural and racial histories analytically, comparatively, experientially. Each can be expected to develop the capacities to engage the complexity of competing truths.

- Because our graduates are part of a society in which ethnic divisions and racial inequities are endemic, they need studies which cultivate understanding of the sources of these divisions and studies that explore competing principles for addressing divisions and inequities.

- Because issues of cultural diversity and racial inequity go directly to the core of human identity and self-knowledge, students should encounter these topics affectively as well as intellectually, learning to draw on experience and human empathy as well as rationality and analysis.

- Because participants in United States society turn to our inherited traditions of democratic aspiration and pluralism for principles to guide their exploration of diversity and equity, students need opportunities to study these traditions in their full complexity, including competing claims, sources, contradictions, injustices, and continuing debates.

- Because it is part of our collective societal tradition to appeal to issues of equity and justice in debates about particulars, students need ways of learning about justice: justice as practice, justice as reasoning, justice as a matrix of aspirations and ideals.

- Because United States communities are part of an increasingly more interdependent world community, students need to locate the United States in its evolving world role and relationships, which requires connections between topics studied as part of United States pluralism and world studies. For increasing numbers of United States students, this may include exploring the world roots of their particular traditions and affiliations.

- Because this society depends, ultimately, on dialogue and deliberation as primary strategies for resolving difference and determining justice, students need extensive opportunities not just to know different communities, cultures, experiences, and aspirations in United States society, but to engage in conversations that explore the differences, connections, and possibilities among human experience and aspiration across our communities.

In short, the multicultural challenges that now engage us cannot be resolved by writing new, more inclusive but still unitary narratives and presenting them to our students as better history and better social science. Rather, we must find ways of helping students learn through engagement with difference, including conflictual, uncongenial forms of human dissent, so that they may construct, together, new affirmations of social reciprocity and ethical obligations.

What curricular strategies can achieve these goals? We should not delude ourselves that a dedicated course or two will adequately prepare our students for a world characterized by multiplicity, inequitable difference, and continuing appeals to principles of justice.

Restructuring our inherited models of education for the public sphere, we need to think in terms of *both dedicated experiences and courses on United States pluralism and an across-the-curriculum approach that teaches students, throughout the whole of their studies, modes of inquiry and forms of engagement appropriate to a world whose hallmark is multiplicity and deep-founded, deep-rooted differences.*

As the American Commitments report *Liberal Learning and the Arts of Connection for the New Academy* recommends, we must commit ourselves to foster:

- grounded selves, capable of connection as well as autonomy;

- dialogues across difference, rather than a rush to identify common ground that some consider comfortable and others a procrustean bed;

- contextualized knowledge that, even as we aspire to truth, recognizes the participatory and communal contexts in which understanding is achieved; and

- developed capacities for living together in a diverse democracy.

Establishing these goals means new emphases in liberal education: new practice in the arts of historicizing, pluralizing, and translating. It means learning to listen and learning to negotiate. It means taking multiplicity as a given and developing competence in working with and through the reality of different traditions, different truths, different levels of trust.

In practice, it means not just the designation of one or two particular courses, but rather an approach that touches the entire curriculum, both general education and major programs, and the still-to-be-created connections between them.

What differentiates our recommended curriculum from school learning and establishes it as an essential curriculum for higher education is its commitment to complexity of thought and knowledge and to deliberative processes. Students should come to this curriculum with a strong grounding in both world and United States history and institutions that they have acquired in the schools. As United States schools begin to meet higher standards for history, students will come to college with greater knowledge of those subjects and will thus be better able to achieve the advanced understanding and capacities that are the goal of our recommendations. But the strengthening of school standards in United States and world history should not be viewed as a substitute for the curriculum we recommend here. Collegiate studies in American pluralism have distinctive and crucial obligations to fulfill: the development of self and societal knowledge that is intrinsic to higher learning and the exploration, in complexity and in depth, of core themes and multiple standpoints in the contested history and unfolding future of United States democratic and cultural pluralism.

CHAPTER FIVE

CURRICULAR RECOMMENDATIONS

Wˢ e recommend that preparation for meaningful citizenship in the United States today be addressed through multiple forms of learning, and, in a variety of educational contexts, across the college experience. Each student's education should include explorations of the following:

1. EXPERIENCE, IDENTITY, AND ASPIRATION: The study of one's own particular inherited and constructed traditions, identity communities, and significant questions, in their complexity.

2. UNITED STATES PLURALISM AND THE PURSUITS OF JUSTICE: An extended and comparative exploration of diverse peoples in this society, with significant attention to their differing experiences of United States democracy and the pursuits—sometimes successful, sometimes frustrated—of equal opportunity.

3. EXPERIENCES IN JUSTICE SEEKING: Encounters with systemic constraints on the development of human potential in the United States and experiences in community-based efforts to articulate principles of justice, expand opportunity, and redress inequities.

4. MULTIPLICITY AND RELATIONAL PLURALISM IN MAJORS, CONCENTRATIONS, AND PROGRAMS: Extensive participation in forms of learning that foster sustained exploration of and deliberation about contested issues important in particular communities of inquiry and practice.

Taken together, these complementary forms of learning—personal, societal, participatory, dialogical—constitute a strong curriculum for diversity and democracy. The forms of learning we recommend here take it as a given that students must learn to grapple, in every part of their learning, with multiplicity, ambiguity, and irreducible differences as defining conditions in the contemporary world.

In almost every culture, the most intimate identities a person carries are learned in the home. It is in the *natio* (the Latin word whence the English word "nation" derives), in one's natal community, often marked and bounded as a sacred space, that humans first gain their sense of relatedness

EXPERIENCE, IDENTITY, AND ASPIRATION

Taken together, these complementary forms of learning—personal, societal, participatory, dialogical—constitute a strong curriculum for diversity and democracy.

to their deities, to their ancestors, and to their kin. The place of birth is where one is habituated to the tastes and smells of the culture called "home"; it is in the home that the "mother tongue" is learned. What is a boy and what is a girl, what obligations the young owe the old, and how the weak relate to the strong gain their first definition in the home. There, too, the children begin to formulate notions of that to which they themselves may aspire.

The home is often the site and locale where the categories that bind natal communities and constitute them as communities of identity are naturalized and imagined as the general order of things, whether in the United States of America, or in other places around the globe. Children, women and the powerless are habitually told by elders, men and others in power that things are the way they are because they have always been that way.

It is in the movement away from home and its naturalized category, through contact with other universes, with people who are unlike us, that the existence, distinctiveness, and particularities of one's own gender, sexual, ethnic, racial, and class identity are revealed. "What are you?" is the crucial question that jolts one from imagining oneself as the center of the universe and into the recognition that other universes daily define, delimit, and constrain our own. Sociologist Mary Waters (1990) maintains that for the majority of children currently living in the United States of America, this unique interrogation begins primarily at school, through contact with children who are different. This is what first prompts the questions every parent inevitably hears: Who are we? Where did we come from? Why and how are we different?

It is at college, however, that students often learn to devalue their cultures. Universities teach them to forget their particularities and local cultures. New aspirations and hopes may replace those the students brought with them from home. Sometimes that process of erasure is accelerated when the institution not only omits study of their traditions but fails to challenge negative cultural stereotypes and media caricatures.

Education for diversity requires that we encourage, rather than discourage, the exploration of origins and identity as a fundamental subject for college study. Students must learn to understand the metaphorical place of their birth and how that place and the specific identities rooted in it fit into a historically textured matrix of social relations. Their new-found aspirations will be stronger as students are encouraged to consciously mediate between the old and the new in their own lives. We often hear faculty members lament that their students know so little of other peoples. It is equally true that they know too little about themselves and of the communities that helped form them. We see such explorations—and students' dialogues with one another about them—as essential in the quest for wisdom.

In large institutions these explorations will be effectively supported by dedicated curricula, for example, courses or programs on Irish history, African American experience, Chicano history, women's studies, religious studies, and the like. Wherever possible, and in ways appropriate to their missions, universities and colleges should encourage the development of programs that provide a scholarly foundation for the study of diverse traditions and experiences, in their distinctive particularities and their intersections.

In smaller institutions, explorations of experience and identity can be undertaken as part of courses with more general titles: a core course on the American Experience in which each student develops and shares an ethnic autobiography; a general first year writing course in which each student is encouraged to do a family narrative; or a humanities course in which all students research and write studies of their individual families' evolving sense of place and connection. One institution with many immigrant students offers a world studies unit on "Journeys," with each student required to study the meaning of cultural encounter and translation and to write a paper about "journeys" in their families' collective memory. Another primarily white institution begins its diversity studies by exploring the concept of homogeneity and then challenging students' perceptions of homogeneity through studies of economic, cultural, and religious differences in middle America.

Guiding Principles

Whatever the specific curricular strategy, the important point is that every student be encouraged to discover his or her identity as a distinctive construction of multiple strands of experience and memory.

We do not assume that ethnic studies are for "minority" students, women's studies for women students, and so forth. Nor do we assume that most students are formed in unitary traditions. Rather, we believe that what has often been a tacit curriculum in United States higher education—the exploration of self, values, meanings, and commitments—ought to become a publicly acknowledged and accredited dimension in every student's education and in the shared discourse of students and faculty in educational communities.

Similarly, we believe that institutions must recognize that liberal education should not seek to sever students from their original connections. Education should indeed be transformative. But the transformations reconstruct and redirect personal and cultural meanings students bring with them from their communities of origin. It is not a victory when students abandon their "parochial" origins if old ties are not rewoven into new fabrics of meaning and significance. Cultural connections are critical dimensions in the experience of liberal learning. They should not be suppressed or denied as the price of admission to the society of well-educated persons. Neither, however, should they be necessarily foregrounded in the first year college experience; institutions should provide flexibility so that students may take up this exploration of self and cultural connection as their own readiness inclines them.

Whatever the specific curricular strategy, the important point is that every student be encouraged to discover his or her identity as a distinctive construction of multiple strands of experience and memory.

EXPERIENCE, IDENTITY, AND ASPIRATION: COURSE DESCRIPTIONS

Most institutions offer dozens of ways that students can explore the complexities of their societal history and identity. Here is a sampling of possibilities from institutions that have been leaders in establishing diversity in the curriculum.

Example A: At the University of Michigan–Ann Arbor, in the course "Writing about Cultural Communities, Ethnicity, and Imposed Categories," students use StorySpace, a hypertext writing tool, to explore and understand the role of cultural background, ethnicity, stereotypes, and other constructed categories by examining their own cultural, ethnic, and historical backgrounds, assessing their own world views, and defining their own cultural agendas. Students write daily, producing a variety of short and medium-length writings, in addition to three substantial hypertext documents. The seminar fulfills the Introductory Composition requirement as well as the Race or Ethnicity requirement.

Example B: In "Cross-Cultural Awareness," offered by the Department of Social Welfare at the University of California–Los Angeles, students explore their own cultural background, including race and ethnicity, to understand better the foundation and roots of their values and how they influence behavior in social and professional interactions. The first assignment consists of the development of a personal cultural autobiography. Students also learn how to practice an ethnographic interview and to develop a cultural lens through which to view a variety of sociological phenomena.

Example C: At the University of Massachusetts–Boston, the Anthropology and American Studies Departments co-sponsor a course entitled "Childhood in America," the main purpose of which is to deconstruct, historically and socioculturally, United States notions of children and childhood both across historical time and across sociocultural groups. A course in which the pedagogy is as carefully thought through as the syllabus, it encourages the student to analyze his or her own childhood and family history in the light of the issues and questions the course raises about American childhoods and American culture. Student essays often discuss new realizations of ignorance about differences, racism, exploitation, or family difficulties. The instructor reports that "many white students…confess they had been ignorant of the struggles of people of color and other minorities, or are ashamed of what the society has allowed," and "many straight students…express shame and regret over their homophobia."

Example D: Four instructors team-teach Seattle Central Community College's "Speaking for Ourselves: Cross-Cultural Visions and Connections." The program uses the disciplines of art, art history, sociology, history, literature, and writing to create a multicultural discourse and vision through which cross-cultural presentations and perceptions of self are examined. How do people define and present themselves? What histories have been created or denied to reflect these social relationships? Questions such as these are brought to bear on experiences of American Indians, West Africans, Asian Americans, and Latino Americans in the United States. The aim is to build self-knowledge and respect for multicultural voices.

Example E: Occidental College requires a substantial commitment (half of the course load in the fall of the freshman year; one course in the spring; eight more courses before the end of the junior year) to its Cultural Studies Program which, taken as a whole, engages students in a wide variety of cultures, experiences, and issues. In the first year, students can select from a range of cultural studies colloquia. "Women of Color in the United States" relies on a reconstruction of knowledge that moves away from the conceptualization of women of color as "other," taking these women's vast and varied experiences as an essential resource and focus for study. Gender, race, and socioeconomic class are presented as central theoretical constructs and as conditions of experience that affect all people. In a colloquium centered on the city of Los Angeles, the city's myths and realities are explored, along with the ways in which they reflect the larger issues of United States culture. A student's interest in science is contextualized in "Technology and Culture," which surveys the relationship between technology and other aspects of culture in four regions of the globe from the early middle ages until the beginning of the modern era. The course especially considers adaptation to the environment, political economy, world view, religion, and aesthetic sensibilities, beginning and ending with considerations of the problems and prospects of Southern California today. "The Great Migrations" looks at different patterns of migration, emigration, and immigration throughout the world, again focusing on, among other areas, the West Coast population, especially Chicanos and Asian Americans. Through these experiences, students learn to locate themselves and to understand those of differing heritage.

UNITED STATES PLURALISM AND THE PURSUITS OF JUSTICE

Courses in United States pluralism and the pursuits of justice should address democratic aspirations and multiple and comparative narratives of participation in United States society.

We live in a culturally diverse society whose peoples do not know one another's cultures and do not know how to learn from one another's traditions. We live in a democracy whose peoples rarely engage either democracy's core principles or one another's different and disparate struggles for justice within the framework of United States democracy. The academy has an opportunity to address both these weaknesses in ways that fulfill its obligation to refract and critically engage the larger society.

We recommend that every college and university require as part of its general education program at least one comparative and relational course in United States pluralism and the pursuits of justice. Because they serve an important civic function and because so many college students take only a year or two toward their degrees, these courses should be offered in the first two years of college or university study. Some institutions may develop a single required course; others may follow the path of establishing criteria and approving a range of courses that meet the criteria.

Guiding Principles

Courses in United States pluralism and the pursuits of justice should present multiple and comparative narratives of participation in United States society. Such courses should deal comparatively and historically with race, gender, ethnicity, class, religion, and other sources of inclusion and exclusion important in this country's history. The central assignments students undertake in such courses should make it impossible to avoid the multiplicity of United States societal experience.

Courses in United States pluralism and the pursuits of justice should also include analysis of United States democratic aspirations and values, engage diverse strands in the history of democratic pluralism, and recognize multivalent understandings of both the meanings and the effects of this country's democratic ideals. Students should have substantial opportunities to explore the pluralism inherent in the term "pursuits" of justice in United States history and contemporary society.

These courses should also encourage extended and collaborative dialogue about the past, present, and future of United States democratic aspirations; cultivate awareness of the enriching aspects of cultural diversity; foster respect for the integrity of other peoples' life experiences; and develop understanding of the multiple vocabularies with which students' neighbors and fellow citizens interpret their lives.

It is especially important that such courses be both comparative and relational. Comparisons open students to multiple experiences of United States society; relational studies provide ways of deliberately connecting one's own perspectives with those of other peoples. Engagement, relation, connection are central pedagogical strategies for courses that prepare students for a deliberative democracy.

American Commitments recommends the establishment of core courses on United States pluralism and the pursuits of justice, through which students become knowledgeable about the struggles toward equality and full participation in which many groups within our country have been and are engaged. Most of the courses described here are graduation requirements for students at these institutions.

Example A: A critical examination of diversity is central to the general education program at LeMoyne-Owen College. Social sciences and humanities classes directly target issues of cultural pluralism and unequal power within both the American and the global context. The six-hour social science sequence "Power and Society" and "Uses and Abuses of Power" explore issues of pluralism and diversity in America and abroad. This includes an examination of racial, ethnic, gender, and class differences, seen largely through the prisms of justice and the distribution of power. The first course emphasizes social and economic disparities, the second cultural and psychological elements. Students in this historically black college also take another six-hour sequence, "African American Heritage," that surveys history from the African background to the present, with particular attention placed on the interaction of the Africans with other cultural groups they encounter, including Europeans and European Americans, American Indians, and Asian Americans.

Example B: As part of a substantial core curriculum program, students at Temple University are required to take one course in American Culture and another in Studies on Race. The aim of the American culture component is to provide students with fundamental, systematic information about the evolution of such ideas as equality of opportunity, "classlessness," social mobility, tolerance, individualism, equality under the law, the United States as a "nation of immigrants," and the United States as a society that welcomes all peoples. Students can compare courses emphasizing those themes with those in Studies on Race, which engage them in a critical examination of knowledge about the existence of racism cross-culturally, historically, and in the United States today. This examination of the effects of racism on individuals and societies helps prepare students to live in a multiracial, multicultural world.

Example C: The purpose of the State University of New York–Buffalo's course "American Pluralism and the Search for Equality" is to examine the multicultural, multiethnic nature of American society from the viewpoints of both men and women and of people of diverse ethnicities, social classes, and religious creeds. Its strategies include two major elements. First, it aims at providing students with increased self-awareness of what it means in our culture to be a person of their own gender, race, class, ethnicity, and religion, as well as an understanding of how these categories affect those who are different from themselves. For example, one instructor uses full-length autobiographies from a variety of writers, finding that reading such works helps students to think better about implications for their own identities. Second, the students are to become more intellectually aware of the causes and effects of structured inequalities and prejudicial exclusion in the United States and of processes leading to a more equitable society.

Example D: "Racial and Ethnic Minorities," devised by a University of Massachusetts–Amherst instructor visiting Wesleyan University, introduces a critical sociological approach to understanding race and ethnicity in the United States, examining how colonialism and immigration have differentially shaped various groups' access to power as part of an explanation of why racism remains an enduring social problem. A study of impediments to the notion of the United States as a "mecca for diversity" includes exploring the interlocking influences of race, class, and gender, and how these intersections manifest themselves in the economy, education, the family, the arts, the law, and other key United States institutions. Throughout the course, special attention is paid to how people create strategies for constructive social change.

COMBINATIONS OF RECOMMENDATIONS 1 AND 2: COURSE DESCRIPTIONS

Especially effective, the American Commitments Panel believes, are courses that combine the grounding of students in their own backgrounds with education in struggles toward justice. These examples suggest two approaches to that goal.

Example A: In the Cultural Foundations segment of the general education curriculum at Saint Edward's University, students taking "The American Experience" first locate themselves as specifically as possible in the many streams of American culture through the writing of their family history. In order to understand the origin and evolution of the values, myths, ideals, and realities that comprise American culture and the multiplicity of influences that have shaped it over time, students are involved in replicating as closely as possible the actual experiences of the "incoming" groups that have shaped and been shaped by the American experience. Another course, "American Dilemmas," continues the theme of social pluralism and consideration of political and social ideals as it explores the problems and issues our society faces in the present. Students are encouraged to address the meaning of individual and public responsibility and to come to grips with conflicting values in defining problems and their solutions.

Example B: Fairleigh Dickinson University has established a core of four courses for undergraduates that examines Western perspectives, exploring a host of issues that, in the past, were seldom explored in traditional Western civilization courses. Readings for "Perspectives on the Individual" reflect the recognition that the issue of multicultural perspectives can be adequately addressed only when voices from cultures throughout the world and considerations of gender and race are included. "The American Experience" moves from a reading of such texts of the American tradition as the Bill of Rights, the Declaration of Independence, and King's "I Have A Dream" speech to the asking of essential questions: Who are "all men"? What is the basis of individual rights? Are we a religious people? What is the American dream and who is included in it? In the third course, "Cross-Cultural Perspectives," the focus is an exploration of the patterns of the traditional cultures of Nigeria, Mexico, India, and China, and the ways in which Western ideas relate to them. Finally, in "Global Issues," social problems such as AIDS, nuclear warfare, and environmental pollution are addressed in ways that go beyond the limits of any one culture or society.

EXPERIENCES IN
JUSTICE SEEKING

An essential ingredient of

an education for democracy

involves, as it did

for the Founding Fathers,

an encounter—successful

or unsuccessful—with the

systemic constraints

on the full flowering

of the human potential.

The study of United States pluralism and the pursuits of justice will help students learn about the worth and tremendous vitality of the diverse peoples of our land, and, in many cases, the structural impediments to the realization of their democratic aspirations. In our judgment, an essential ingredient of an education for democracy involves, as it did for the Founding Fathers, an encounter—successful or unsuccessful—with the systemic constraints on the full flowering of the human potential. Without this encounter, the study of United States history and society will remain theoretical, cerebral, abstract, and uninvolved.

We call these encounters with systemic constraints "experiences in the pursuits of justice." The inclusion of these pursuits in our curricular recommendations is intended to immerse the student in the experience of justice seeking, of leveling the playing field. Such experiences, in their very conception, would involve students in working with communities and locales where the promises of democracy have been most denied or half-heartedly implemented.

These experiences in justice seeking, it should be emphasized, overlap with but are intended to be quite different from traditional (though still too rare) opportunities for service to the community. While community-service opportunities might focus on providing needed care or on bridging theory and practice, these justice-seeking internships focus more directly on making democracy work for those groups for whom it has worked comparatively poorly. Essential for us is only the immersion of the student in the efforts—sometimes successful, sometimes frustrated, sometimes short-term, sometimes long-term—in pursuit of equal opportunity.

Different institutions and different communities, of course, will define the pursuit of justice differently. This curricular recommendation encourages, therefore, a mutually respectful dialogue between (on the one hand) college or departmental authorities and (on the other) community leadership in defining a mutually attractive agenda.

What are some examples of the kind of experience we are recommending? The list which follows is meant to suggest the range of such experiences; but we stress again that each locale must evolve its own list:

- assisting teachers in underfunded or poorly equipped high schools with mathematics or basic science instruction for at-risk students;

- working to understand and to change patterns of residential discrimination with community residents, public housing authorities, local banks, and urban planners;

- working as volunteers or interns with politically focused organizations like United We Stand, the Rainbow Coalition, the Southern Coalition for Economic and Social Justice;

EXPERIENCES IN JUSTICE SEEKING: COURSE DESCRIPTIONS

While many institutions encourage community service, it is less common to integrate service learning into the curriculum. These institutions have established courses that serve as useful models.

Example A: Pitzer College's social responsibility requirement stipulates that students complete a semester of social service community work through a course internship, an independent study, or a non-credit community service assignment. The intent is to provide students with the experience of working with and on behalf of others and to encourage reflection upon the ethical implications of their actions. For example, in the course titled "Social Responsibility and Community," students participate as observers, mentors, and teacher aides in two local multiethnic school districts. From the course has emerged a project through which Pitzer students assist high school teachers and administrators in addressing incidents of interethnic conflict in their schools and developing multicultural and conflict resolution programs. The course "Violence in Intimate Relationships" involves students in working as interns in a shelter or other appropriate agency that serves battered women or abused children.

Example B: In the Hobart and William Smith Colleges course "Politics, Community, and Service," students focus on the meaning of citizenship in an intercultural society. They are required to engage in ten hours of community work at sites approved by the instructor and community partners, and directly related to issues raised in the course. There are extensive readings in the areas of social difference, inequality, social justice, and democratic citizenship. Students keep a journal outlining their reaction to the assigned authors as well as a chronicle of their field experiences and community involvement.

Example C: Rutgers University's Civic Education and Community Service Program offers a number of courses integrating community service and classroom work in a variety of fields. "Performing Artists" includes work in the schools, such as after-school drama and dance programs. Experience in the community informs and is informed by the academic segment of the course, evoking questions concerning the role of the performing artist in a democratic society, and social responsibility in the arts. "HIV and Society," offered in conjunction with a biology course, provides a forum to apply that course work in the exploration of questions of public health, policy options and consequences, community awareness as related to issues surrounding HIV, and social responsibilities to others. Students also take part in HIV-related community services.

- interning with local community service agencies, tribal agencies, or local banks, or with community outreach departments of large urban corporations on long-range economic-development plans;

- teaching in local prisons to assist inmates in obtaining their high-school equivalency degrees or in learning computer skills or a foreign language;

- assisting in voter registration drives;

- creating and organizing the long-term staffing of child-care facilities for parents who are just returning to school or to the work force; and

- developing and presenting a community history of justice seeking for use in local libraries.

Guiding Principles

Innovations such as this run the risk of being perceived as marginal add-ons to the central business of a college education. For the sake of reinforcing our commitment to the importance of such experiences, we offer these guiding principles to those who may be charged with creating such initiatives:

- Throughout this report we have been emphasizing the importance of educating our students to the values and practice of democracy. These experiences in justice seeking are intended to be an experiential introduction to the ways in which democracy works or fails to work, for the sake of making our students more effective contributors to the realization of democratic values.

- While there is some value in virtually any involvement with the practical or daily concerns of the local community, our judgment is that the experiences most educative and illuminating for our students are those which immerse them in the justice-seeking aspirations of the groups especially ill-served by the current configurations of economic and social opportunity.

- To enable the students to be useful participants in the community's effort, the institution or department must integrate the preparation and supervision of the student's participation into the curriculum and into the workload of the faculty.

- Lest the experience be fragmented, the institution or the department must integrate opportunities for reflection, discussion, and feedback into the effort. This reflection might take many forms, for example, bi-weekly seminars on progress or lack thereof, a senior-level integrative paper which relates disciplinary theory to practice, a presentation to the city council, etc.

- It is essential that each college work collaboratively *from the start* with local groups (official or disenfranchised) in defining a mutually attractive agenda. There ought not to be the slightest hint of the college's or the department's imposing an agenda or a favored solution upon the community. The experience of working with a highly diverse group of people, perhaps from different cultures from the students, in the forging of a common agenda, is in our judgment an essential component of the liberal education appropriate to multicultural democracy.

Gerald Graff (1992) has popularized the exhortation "teach the conflicts." We expand and broaden that recommendation to encompass teaching students how to engage conflictual difference or, more precisely, how to participate in collective deliberations about issues where different participants do not agree and are not likely ever to reach unitary understanding. Optimally, such explorations will involve students in experience-based as well as classroom learning and in opportunities to learn from, as well as contribute to, communities of practice related to their central interests. Necessarily, these explorations must involve students in situations where different cultural expectations, competing principles, and different perceptions of the good come into play.

Developing capacities for relational pluralism might fruitfully culminate in an interdisciplinary advanced course in which students discover the potential complementarities, as well as the disjunctures, among different ways of framing and exploring a topic. But teaching the arts of learning through difference is not the work of a single course and certainly not the work of a single course taken late in a course of study. Rather, the capacities basic to relational pluralism are effectively nurtured across a set of extended studies, through a curriculum in which students have multiple opportunities to work in disparate kinds of groups, to explore topics from multiple points of view, to experience others' strongly felt convictions, to take multiple perspectives and convictions into account in forming their own interpretations, and to acknowledge honestly and dialogically the points and positions at which others will take significant exception to their own observations, interpretations, judgments, and conclusions.

The arts and capacities important to relational pluralism may be introduced in the studies we recommend on experience, identity, and aspiration and on United States pluralism and the pursuits of justice. But students will develop competence in these arts only if major programs build on the introductions provided through general education, fostering the practices of relational pluralism in ways appropriate to their subjects and *significant to students who choose to study in specific fields*.

MULTIPLICITY AND RELATIONAL PLURALISM IN MAJORS, CONCENTRATIONS, AND PROGRAMS

The differences students engage in their major studies may be cultural; they may be perspectival or experiential; they may be discipline- or context-related. They may, where possible, include issues of justice and reciprocal obligation. Students can encounter multiplicity and difference through projects, through technology-based dialogues, through linked courses that juxtapose differing approaches to a common topic.

The important thing is that programs and departments involve students in extensive opportunities to practice deliberative discourse on subjects about which they care intensely. All graduates in all programs must learn to listen to others' experiences and challenges, explore multiple ways of knowing and forming knowledge, and open themselves to experiences of modifying their own understandings based on what they have learned from others' contributions.

Students' encounters with diversity through major programs—acknowledging complexity and multiplicity, exploring the dimensions of difference, taking multiplicity into full account in their own constructions—further the deliberative *practice* of United States pluralism. Students learn to listen to one another in order to understand more completely. Equally important, through their immersion in topics where no single perspective can be adequate to the complexity of the issue, students discover both the limitations of any particular framework and, by extension, their inescapable dependence on difference as a source of greater understanding.

Students discover both the limitations of any particular framework and, by extension, their inescapable dependence on difference as a source of greater understanding.

MULTIPLICITY AND RELATIONAL PLURALISM IN MAJORS, CONCENTRATIONS, PROGRAMS: EXAMPLES

In this final category we call not only for individual course work, but also for an infusion, across the curriculum, of knowledge and skills in negotiating diversity. Even those institutions most deeply involved with diversity issues would not yet claim that all their curricular and co-curricular programs are completely transformed to take into account the multiplicity of persons and perspectives that comprise them. We look here at initiatives that move in the direction of infusion and at strategies that seem to promise real progress. It is helpful to make a clear distinction between adding content on diversity topics to the curriculum and deliberately cultivating skills in negotiating differences that cannot or should not be assimilated.

I. ENGAGING DIFFERENCE: COURSE WORK

Example A: Clustering courses is a useful way of extending the intellectual engagement with diversity over a broader spectrum than can be accomplished with a single course, as well as providing a more integrated learning experience. A course cluster developed at the State University of New York–Potsdam illustrates the way linked courses can help students work through multiple points of view. Three instructors created the cluster, called "Becoming American," drawing on courses from politics, English, and anthropology. Ronald Takaki's *A Different Mirror: A History of Multicultural America* serves as the centerpiece around which the texts for the three courses are grouped. Instructors report that this approach helps students apply their learning across courses with greater facility. The politics course, "United States Pluralism and the Pursuits of Justice," examines how United States government policy has affected people of color and identified some of the cultural values inherent in American law. "Women in American Indian Cultures," the anthropology component, looks at the impact of government policy on the lives of American Indian women and how the narrative about them was framed by anthropologists. Meanwhile, through the literature course, "Dragons, Ghosts, and China Dolls," students gain a knowledge of the canon of Chinese American women's literature and consider questions of Chinese American female identity through the intersections of gender, race, class, and ethnicity.

Example B: An introductory course in the English department at the University of Chicago engages students in contested issues within the field through exposure to the department's diverse perspectives and methods. Each section of the course is taught by an instructor in the required course for majors, "Methodologies and Issues of Literary Study." The several sections are taught concurrently so that the classes may come together periodically for shared meetings on topics related to the assigned texts. These meetings provide a forum for students to experience intraprofessional differences, as well as the differences between professional and student viewpoints. Gerald Graff, one of the course instructors, notes that, "if introduced properly, the faculty perspectives can create a context for studying the primary literature rather than crowding it out, and students can acquire a map of the department and, by extension, of the field."

Example C: At Loyola University in Chicago, the department of communications requires all majors to take an introductory course which examines communication practices in light of the social, historical, and political contexts which have shaped them. Students explore the relationships between communication practices and questions of social power, knowledge, world view, aesthetics, and action. Additionally, the department offers a social justice concentration. Among the required courses is an internship or directed study, in which service, academic study, and structured reflection are deliberately linked; sample sites include Urban League, Philippine Workers Alliance, Coalition for Homeless, and PTAs. An introductory course, "Social Justice and Communication," explores ways that communication can serve social justice by assisting those concerned with poverty and inequality.

II. ENGAGING DIFFERENCE: CO-CURRICULAR STRATEGIES

Hobart and William Smith Colleges are actively working with diversity issues at the co-curricular level. They have instituted a Community Service House for students committed to performing five hours of service per week. The house coordinates efforts between school and community, and sponsors dialogue groups among students where they learn the skills of articulation, mediation, conflict resolution, and positive action around issues of interculturalism and pluralism.

CONCLUSION

In the other reports in this series, we have recommended that higher education commit itself to cultivating capacities for associated living as an important outcome of higher education. What would be the outcome of such a commitment? What marks would we look for in successful graduates of this recommended curriculum?

Here are possibilities. Envision a group of Americans, different in background and economic resources. They are vigorously debating a contentious societal issue, perhaps the justice of limiting welfare support to three years as a lifetime maximum. Each is listening carefully, without interrupting, to what the other is saying. Each is able to explain why other members of the group see the issues as they do. Each can describe how different histories and affiliations have shaped participants' different understandings. Each spends a great deal of time considering the effects of particular policies on different cases: the hardworking legal immigrant parent whose efforts to be self-sufficient are hindered by a poor labor market and employment preference for United States citizens; the drug addict who is not really available to work; the teenage mother with a sickly child. No one attacks the motives, intelligence, or worth of anyone else in the conversation. No one applies a principle without considering its implications. Several people in the group have had family experiences or field studies that involved them in welfare issues; they bring a base of experience to the discussion.

By the time the discussion ends, every participant in the dialogue has recast at least part of his or her original position in light of insights and opposing views offered in the conversation. The group has decided on the points where agreement has to be reached and spent the most time on those points. They have also acknowledged issues where continued disagreement must be accepted. Every participant can readily explain how the several histories and perspectives reflected in the group improved the quality of their own and others' thinking.

How is this different from traditional aspirations for liberal and general education? In principle, not very. What is different is the practice. Participants in this imaginary dialogue are respectful of one another's perspectives and the histories that shape them. They are attuned to the complexities of making a just and workable policy. They know the topic experientially as well as analytically. And they have had extensive experience in confronting multiplicity and negotiating deep-rooted difference.

We invite our colleagues around the country to discuss these recommendations in groups that reflect the range of United States diversities.

Most significantly, they recognize that their thinking is pushed, deepened, and eventually strengthened by the diversity of the group. They do not all agree with one another on the issues under discussion and are never likely to reach complete agreement. But every one of them believes, on the basis of experience, that the diverse backgrounds and perspectives represented in the group add to the quality of their insight and understanding. No one of them would choose to discuss the subject without the benefit of the complex experiential, cultural, and historical perspectives that diversity brings to the table. No one of them would think excellence enhanced if the group could become less diverse—and less complex.

We are, of course, far from reaching this state of deliberative pluralism. We have scarcely begun to envision it. But as we move away from celebrating diversity and into the harder work of what many call "difficult dialogues," we must also ask where we want to go. What future are we trying to shape?

The American Commitments recommendations for diversity in the curriculum envision a different way of relating to, learning from, working with, and valuing one another. We invite our colleagues around the country to discuss these recommendations in groups that reflect the range of United States diversities. What kinds of communities do we seek to create? And what kind of education do we need—for ourselves as well as our students—to move us closer to our aspirations?

WORKS CITED

Appleby, Joyce Oldham. 1992. *Liberalism and republicanism in the historical imagination*. Boston: Harvard University Press.

Association of American Colleges and Universities. 1985. *Integrity in the college curriculum: A report to the academic community*. Washington, D.C.: Association of American Colleges and Universities.

Graff, Gerald. 1992. *Beyond the culture wars: How teaching the conflicts can revitalize American education*. New York and London: W.W. Norton and Company.

Hamilton, Alexander. 1982. Federalist 70. In *The Federalist Papers*. Edited by Gary Wills. New York: Bantam Books.

Justiz, M. J., R. Wilson, and L. G. Björk. 1994. *Minorities in higher education*. Phoenix: Oryx Press.

Karen, David. 1991. The politics of class, race, and gender: Access to higher education in the United States, 1960–1986. *American Journal of Education* 99 (2): 208–237.

Massey, Douglas S., and Nancy A. Denton. 1993. *American apartheid: Segregation and the making of the underclass*. Cambridge, Mass.: Harvard University Press.

Rudolph, Frederick. 1977. *Curriculum: A history of the American undergraduate course of study since 1636*. San Francisco, Washington, D.C., and London: Jossey-Bass Publishers.

Schmitz, Betty. 1992. *Core curriculum and cultural pluralism: A guide for campus planners*. Washington, D.C.: Association of American Colleges and Universities.

Searle, John. 1993. Is there a crisis in American higher education? *Partisan Review* 60 (4): 693–709.

Smith, Daryl G. 1995. Organizational implications of diversity in higher education. In *Diversity in organizations*. Edited by M. Chemers, S. Oskamp, and M. Costanza. Newbury Park, Calif.: Sage Publications.

Sunstein, Cass. 1992. Free speech now. In *The Bill of Rights in the modern state*. Edited by G. R. Stone, R. A. Epstein, and C. R. Sunstein. Chicago: University of Chicago Press.

———. 1993. *The partial Constitution*. Cambridge, Mass.: Harvard University Press.

Takaki, Ronald. 1993. *A different mirror*. Boston: Little, Brown.

Waters, Mary C. 1990. *Ethnic options: Choosing identities in America.* Berkeley, California: University of California Press.

West, Cornel. 1994. Race and social justice in America. *Liberal Education* 80 (3): 32–39.

The data in the foreword on the racial recomposition in United States urban areas was compiled by Troy Duster, professor of sociology, University of California–Berkeley.

Eileen O'Brien of Policy Studies Associates, Inc., in Washington, D.C., compiled the data in the foreword on the educational participation and attainment of various ethnic groups.